THE MAGICAL

AMULET BAG

Volume 2

by

Sigrid Wynne-Evans

Illustrations by

Lori Berry and Sigrid Wynne-Evans

Wynne-Evans, Sigrid, 1956-

The Magical Amulet Bag/ by Sigrid Wynne-Evans
ISBN # 09648360-2-5

CREDITS

Ralph Allen Thanks again for the great photography. Your ideas are always amusing as well as helpful. Those evenings in cyber space together have given me a lot of laughs. You are a very dear friend.

Linda Benmour Thanks for your encouragement, and help in picking out the photographs.

Lori Berry For help in pulling it all together, and with the page layout. Thanks for all the encouragement.

Jasmine For putting up with my time on the computer, and all those classes. She is my constant support and best friend as well as my daughter.

Toni, Beth and Cindi at THREE BEADS AND A BUTTON, Cupertino, CA. Hey ladies, you've got a great store that keeps getting better. Thanks for encouraging my creativity!!

Karey Navo at JEWELRY CRAFTS MAGAZINE. It's hard to believe that I've written for you for four years. Thanks for all those words of encouragement that always seemed to come when I needed them most.

Absolute Graphics, San Jose CA. You did a great job in designing my cover and color pages.

To all of you who have written There are too many of you to thank individually, but I really appreciate the input and encouragement that each of you have given me.

And finally to all the stores Thank you for carrying my books.

Dear Beaders,

Here is my 6th book, Vol. 2 of The Magical Amulet Bag! I hope that you like these designs. I think this book has even better designs than the first volume.

If you would like to write or send me comments as to what you like (or don't like) about my books, or if you need some help understanding something, please feel free to contact me at the address below.

While I try to answer every letter I get, your reply will be guaranteed if you enclose a stamped return envelope.

If you have ordered from me directly, your name is placed on my mailing list. I will keep you informed on my up coming books as they near completion. If you would like to be on my mailing list, please send me your name and address and I will be happy to include you.

HAPPY BEADING!

Sig

Sig Wynne-Evans
P.O. Box 110894
Campbell, CA 95011
(408) 379-8647

E-Mail: BeadedBear@aol.com

TABLE OF CONTENTS

INTRODUCTION

Amulet bags have become quite popular in recent times. Perhaps it is because the bags are a connection with an era long past. Amulet bags were once the carrier of special powers and protection, the contents of which were only known to the owner. Or perhaps it is because of the elegance and the ease of self expression that these modernized amulet bags allow the maker. Whatever the reason of the popularity of the amulet bags, they are a joy to make and an even greater joy to wear.

Most of the patterns that I have seen for beaded amulet bags are geometric designs. I like the challenge, and the results of a picture in my beadwork, as those of you who've bought my earring pattern books know. The construction of the bags in this book is very simple, there are no fancy shapes or fancy stitches to worry about. The exciting part of the bags in this book are the patterns themselves.

The Basics

There are few materials needed to create the bags in this book. The choices of beads and beading supplies that are available are vast. The correct choices will make the bags beautiful, while the wrong choices may make the bags less than appealing. Therefore, I will attempt to give you a bead primer in hopes that your choices will help you make an amazing bag.

Needle and Thread

The easiest choices that you will have will be the type of needle and thread that you will use. Most of you will choose to use a size 11^0 bead (more about bead sizes later). For this size bead, a size 12 beading needle will do just fine.

Beading needles differ from regular sewing needles in that they are longer and thinner. The eye is narrow and long as compared to a sewing needle. This is an important feature in that the holes in beads are fairly small and you will be passing the needle and thread through the bead more than once.

Beading needles are available in several sizes. Size 12 is the most commonly used. A size 15 needle will be needed for size 14 beads. As with beads, the higher the number, the smaller the diameter of the needle.

"NYMO" beading thread is highly recommended for any type of seed bead work. Do not use regular sewing thread as it has a tendency to fray much too quickly. "NYMO" thread is a nylon thread which is fairly strong and is available in several sizes. My personal preference is to use size O or A. Other beaders like to use size B, which is thicker. Since some Czech beads have quite small holes, even in size 11^0 beads, the B thread may fill up the beads in the base row so that you will not be able to pass through the beads for the completion of the fringe. Therefore, I use the smaller size thread to ensure that I will be able to pass through the bead several times. ⎯⎯⎯⎯

Many beaders like to wax the thread with bee's wax. The wax will help keep the thread from fraying and knotting. I do not wax my thread. Again, this is just a personal preference. I do not like the waxy feel of the thread. Sometimes the wax also builds up on the top of the beads. The wax also adds bulk to the thread which may be just enough to fill up the hole of the bead so that you won't be able to pass through the required amount of times.

While I have given you my own personal preferences as a starting point for your choices of needle and thread, I do not mean to imply that other choices are wrong. Try other choices to see if they work better for you. There really is no single right way, only what works best for you. So experiment!

Beads, Beads, and More Beads

Now, we have reached the fun part!! And also the most difficult in terms of the choices that you will have available to you.

Seed Beads are the basis for the designs in this book. Bugle beads and the small 4mm crystals may be used at the end of the dangles as accents. There is a wide array of seed beads available. A basic knowledge of the different types and styles that are available will help you with your selection of beads for the bags in this book.

Seed beads are packaged for sale in many different ways. Some stores will package beads in small tubes, others will sell them by the hank. On occasion you will also see seed beads packaged by weight. How these beads are sold often depends on how the supplier distributes the beads. So, if you are comparing prices, about the only fair way to compare price is to know the price per kilo or per gram.

Seed beads come in different sizes, the most common sizes are 9^0, 10^0, 11^0, 12^0, 13^0, 14^0, 15^0 and 16^0. Of these, 11^0 is the most widely used.

When working the designs in this book, bead size uniformity is very important. Beads will vary in size within a hank and from manufacturer to manufacturer. I've used 11^0 beads that look more like 10^0, and 11^0 beads that look more like 12^0. Care must be taken in choosing beads!

Size 11^0 will work well for the designs in this book. If you are a beginner, then I would recommend that you start by using size 11^0, simply because you will have more to hold on to. However, I strongly recommend that you use Delica beads. They will make your bag absolutely beautiful.

The number one rule of buying beads is to buy all the beads you will need (or can possibly buy) of the style/color that you intend to use. If you favor certain colors, it may be in your best interest to buy bulk (1/4 kilo or more) because unless you are very organized and lucky, you will either forget where you bought those beads, or the dye lot has changed, or the worst of all possibilities — it is a discontinued color/style. This has happened to me several times. Also, the bead import business or the reliability of the manufacturer may be such that your favorite store is out of that particular bead and it may take 6 months for them to get another shipment.

So, enough about size and on to style.

Seed beads can come in a variety of cuts. Smooth beads have been tumbled to give their surface a regular texture. There are no facets. These are probably what you think of as the typical bead.

Cut seed beads can be found as 2-cuts, 3-cuts, and hex-cuts, with facets on 2, 3, and 6 sides respectively.

Charlotte beads have little facets cut into them on 1 or 2 sides. These beads reflect the light very nicely and can give your piece a very elegant look.

Seed beads also come in a variety of finishes. The most common ones are listed below.

Aurora Borealis (AB), also known as **Iris**, **Iridescent**, or **Fire Polish**: These have a rainbow effect on the surface.

Ceylon: Surface is some what pearlized.

Delica: A laser cut bead in wonderful colors. Highly recommended.

Greasy: This is an "old" finish. It's opaque, but has depth. The colors are very limited. Yellow, turquoise, and green are the most common.

Opaque: Light will not pass through these beads. Sometimes these are referred to as chalky colors.

Transparent: Light passes through these beads, giving your piece a stained glass appearance.

Beads To Beware Of!!!!

Metallic beads look so beautiful. They shine so beautifully and are spectacular in a piece. But alas, how they fade!!

I've used some metallic Czechoslovakian beads in a beautiful fuchsia and a brilliant blue. The bags were spectacular! But two days in the sun made them fade from those lovely colors to wishy washy colors with strong tin color overtones. In short, a disgusting color that no one would like.

Japan is manufacturing some lovely metallics that I've been seduced by. Before I use them in a major project, I'll test them by leaving them out in the sun and by washing them to see how they hold up. Rumor amongst those in the know is that they do last provided that you don't shower with them or use them in areas where perspiration and body oils will degrade them.

Surface dyed beads are another problem bead. If they aren't marked as such, the give away signs are: a mottled appearance on the surface of the bead (uneven color) or the holes will have a tendency to be a tad darker than the surface. I've had some poor quality beads that were pretty enough in their package, but the color rubbed off during the course of working with the piece! Pinks are especially prone to this. So keep your eyes open to this problem.

Color lined beads may also be a problem. These beads have a different color painted in the hole from what the outside color is. Sometimes this inside color can rub off.

CHOOSING COLORS

I have provided a color code for each design in this book. The color codes are only a suggestion or a guide. These colors have worked well for me, but if you wish, try other colors.

From the above discussion on beads, you can see that if the code calls for a "RED" bead, you will still have to choose what type of "RED" bead to use. The choice of color and type of finish of the bead can make or break the design. With the simpler designs, involving 2-3 colors, the choice of beads may not be as critical. Beads with a reasonable contrast will almost always work. However, on complex designs involving 5 or more colors, particularly when 2 or more shades of the same color are used, contrast will become critical.

One of the first lessons in creating designs that are identifiable is that if several colors of transparent beads are used together, they tend to blend in together. For example, light pink with white or pink with lavender. Since the success of the design will depend heavily on the distinction of color changes, you will not want a blending of colors.

When choosing colors, generally I will choose colors that are as distinct as I can possibly find. If you choose your colors by laying hanks of beads together, you may be surprised to find that even if the hanks contrast well, if you were to place one or two beads of each color together, they may be nearly indistinguishable. Always put one or two beads of each color together on a needle if there is any question of whether of not the beads will hold their own distinct color or if the eye will blend them together. This is especially important for transparent beads, although some opaque hues may need this test as well.

Transparent beads are wonderful for background colors, especially if opaque colors are used for the design. Light will pass through the transparent beads making them recess into the background, while the light will stop or reflect back to the eye on the opaque beads used in the design. This type of contrast is strong. Areas requiring a strong definition such as outlines should almost always be done in opaque beads.

An Extra Tip

Uniformity of bead size will always be important. The design and shape of the bag is affected by the beads in it. If all of the beads are not of a uniform size, it will be instantly noticeable. When looking at a hank of beads, you will notice that there is some variation in size. Some may be fat while others may be slivers. Try to choose beads that are fairly uniform.

THE CRAFT BUSINESS

One day many of you will want to venture into business selling your beadwork. When I first began, I had no idea of how to go about selling my beadwork. It took years of research and many hard knocks to learn what I know now. I will give you a few ideas on getting started so that your start won't be as much as a struggle as mine was.

There are several ways in which to sell your beadwork. The most common ways are: 1.) direct sales, such as wholesale and retail; and 2.) consignment. Each of these has endless possibilities.

When you are first starting out, consignment is probably the first opportunity that will come your way. Consignment means that the store will keep your merchandise and will pay you a percentage of the selling price after the piece has sold. Most seasoned craftspeople will not take on consignment accounts because there are some very definite drawbacks. But for the beginner, a consignment account may be a very good opportunity to sell beadwork provided that certain pitfalls are avoided. The main thing that I want to impress upon you is that the store has no risk in consignments. So if you agree to consignments, be sure that YOU set the terms, because if anyone loses it will be you.

Consignment agreements will vary from store to store. Consignment agreements may be 70/30, 60/40, or 50/50. The first number is the percentage of the sale that you will get, the second number is the percentage of the selling price that the store will retain. Be sure to find out if the store will add on their commission to your asking price or if they will subtract their commission from your price. Depending on the answer, you may have to adjust your prices accordingly.

With consignment accounts be sure that you get all the specifics in writing. Have everything spelled out such as: when you will be paid (after each sale or monthly), who is responsible for theft or damage (don't sign the agreement if the store assumes no such liability), what percent of the selling price you are to receive, and how much of a notice will be required of you to pick up your work if you wish to reclaim possession.

Another way to sell beadwork, and in my opinion, a more fun and profitable way, is at Art and Craft Shows. There is a significant investment required before you can participate in a show as you will need to acquire an acceptable display, i.e., canopy, tables and possibly a display case. In addition, some show fees are expensive too. The advantage in participating in the shows is that you are selling at retail cost rather than at wholesale, and the potential for repeat business as well as custom work is high. Also, you may get calls for you work from someone who picked up your card long after the show is over.

Before participating in a show, visit the event to try to get a feel for how well attended it is and try to get an idea if your work would be well received with the clientele. If you're lucky enough to find a beader at the show, try to see if she (he) is willing to share some information with you. While some people are rather tight lipped about the whole process, others are more than willing to try to help.

A word on pricing — a general formula used by many crafters is: Wholesale Price = cost of materials x 3 + hourly wage. While this is a guide, it is not the end all in pricing. Most people forget to consider costs such as gas and time to go to stores to buy supplies, storage equipment, packaging or cards for displays and many other incidental costs. With all things considered, a beaded bag may only cost at most $15 to make, perhaps the most important consideration is the time involved.

I am a rather vocal advocate of beaders getting paid for their artistry. Few of us actually do. Yet there are some beaders who give away their work. This is what angers me. I've seen some beaders who've made my designs and sold them for about $40. I know the time involved. DO NOT SELL THEM SO CHEAPLY!!! My wholesale prices for most of my bags range from $85-$150 depending on the complexity and the type of beads and accents used. My retail prices range from about $150-$250 on most bags. If the store tells you that you are too expensive, then you have not found the right market for your work. Keep looking!!! Those of you who sell too cheaply do a great disservice to the rest of us, and reinforce the idea that beadwork is a "CHEAP" form of art.

Peyote Stitch Directions

Note that the patterns at the end of this book show **only** the **front** of the bag. If you wish, the pattern may be repeated on the back. I leave the back a solid color and "sign" my bags by stitching in my name. I have provided graphs of letters so that you may do the same.

The "start" number given on each graph is the **total** number of beads you need to pick up in order to begin that particular bag. These beads are both row #1 and row #2.

Reading a Graph

In order to follow a graph, you must understand how to read it. Note how the rows are numbered.

Thread a needle with about 1 yard of thread. Thread is used

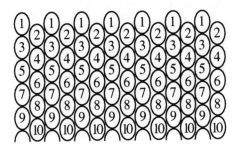

single strength. Begin by picking up the number indicated on the graph. (Remember that when beginning a peyote stitch bag, the start number of beads is both row #1 and row #2. Single bead stitching begins with row #3.) If you are a beginner, and do not wish to follow a graph, pick up 30 beads of one color. Tie the beads into a circle by running the needle through the beads from beginning to end.

Now we begin with the single bead stitching. If you are following the pattern, pick a spot on the graph to begin with. Mark that point with a dot. Pick up colors accordingly. For beginners, use a second color for row #3.

Put a bead on the needle, skip one bead of the circle and go into the next. If you are new to this, it helps to say to yourself "the thread is coming out of bead #1, skip bead #2 and go into bead #3. Continue until you have reached the end of the row.

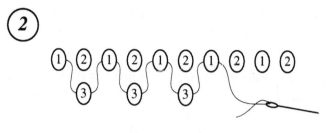

Numbers = row

You have reached the end of the row when you go into the same bead as this row started out of.

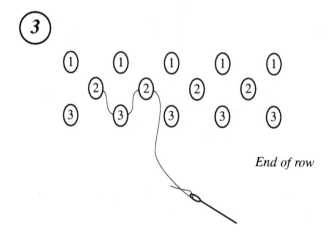

End of row

At this point, you are now ready for the "step down" into row #4. Bring the needle (do not pick up a new bead) through the first bead of row #3.

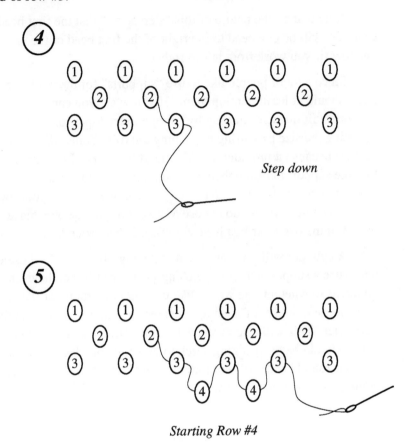

Step down

Starting Row #4

This step down will occur at the end of *each* row. You can sew the last bead of a row and step down in one stitch once you are comfortable with this technique.

Note that by the nature of this "step down" that the first bead of each row will be one bead to the right of the first bead of the previous row (if you work from left to right).

Since a lot of people like to use "supports" for the work, I feel that I should at least mention them. If you wish, you can make a support to fit inside of the bag by using a toilet paper roll and adjusting the size by cutting and taping the roll. Some like to use a support because it provides an aid to hold the work. I personally find the support to be cumbersome and it is just another item for my thread to get caught up in. Whether you use one or not is your own personal choice. If you do choose to do choose to use one, make one to fit the bag after you have completed about four rows.

A cylinder will form as you are beading. If you have chosen not to use a support and you are using Delica beads, you have an option as to whether you would like the bag to be round or flat. If you choose to make it flat, simply center the pattern and squash the beads flat. This will also give a very well defined edge to the bag which should have an edging stitch to make the bag look finished. Regular round beads will not flatten as the Delicas will, therefore an edging stitch will not be necessary.

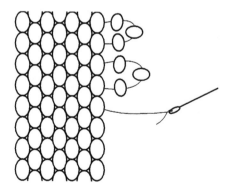

Once the bag is finished, stitch together the beads of the last row in a zipper-like fashion.

Peyote Bag Extensions

Brick Stitch

Several of the bags have design elements that extend beyond the body of the bag. Those extensions that are on the sides of the bag are done in brick stitch. These extensions are added after the body is completed, and before the edging is added.

To begin, you must first create the connecting threads between beads needed for brick stitch. This is done simply by weaving in and out of the edge beads.

①

Pick up one bead, as required by the pattern. Bring the needle and thread, from back to front, under a connecting bead. Then bring the needle up through the added bead to lock it into place.

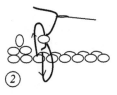

②

To increase the length of the brick stitch is simple. Have your needle coming out of the end bead of the row below the increase as in the illustration. Pick up two beads and stitch as usual. This will increase the row by one bead.

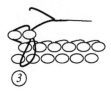

③

If you need to increase the row by more than one bead, or if you need to increase the row that you are presently working on, you will continue to add one bead at a time. For those of you familiar with brick stitch earrings, this is the same idea as the foundation row.

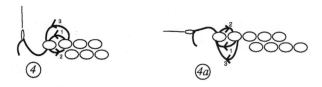

PEYOTE STITCH

Flat peyote stitch is used for the extensions that appear on the top or the bottom of the bags. Whether you add the extension on the bottom of the bag before or after sewing the bottom together, is one of personal preference.

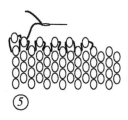

To decrease the area, simply stop short as required by the pattern, or weave back to where you need to be.

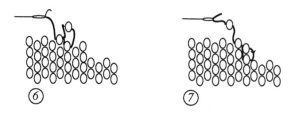

Strap Options

Single Strand Strung Bead Strap

Attach a double thread to the top of the bag. String beads as desired and securely attach thread to the opposite side of the bag. Attach another double thread to the bag and re-thread all of the strap beads for re-enforcement.

- ❑ Try stringing a pattern of 4 seed beads (11^0) and one 6^0 seed bead.
- ❑ Add accent beads such as crystals and fetishes.

Multi Strand Strung Strap

Attach a double thread to the top of the bag. Add a combination of 10 seed beads and one accent bead. Secure thread to opposite side of the bag once the desired length is obtained. With a new double strand of thread, pick up 10 seed beads and go through the accent bead. Repeat to end. Add as many strands as you wish.

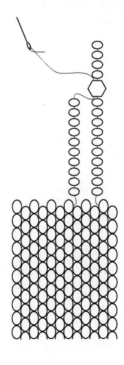

FIGURE 8 STRAP

Attach 2 threads to the top of the bag (double strand). Pick up 4 beads with each needle. Bring right needle through the 4th bead of the left side, and left needle through the 4th bead of the right side.

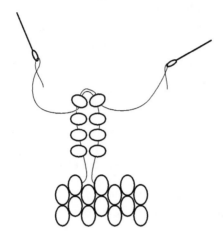

Continue by picking up 4 beads on each needle and crossing over until you've reached the desired length.

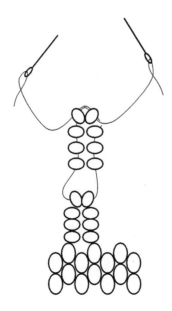

For the last group of beads, pick up 3 beads with each needle and connect to the bag. Weave through several beads for security before knotting.

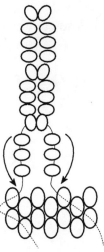

PEYOTE STRAP

Peyote stitched straps are simply an extension of the peyote stitched bag. Make this strap as wide as you wish. You may also wish to incorporate patterns.

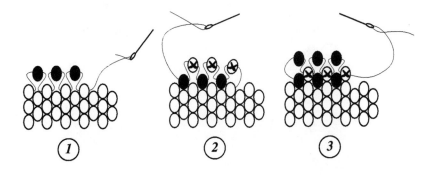

DAISY CHAIN STRAP

1 Tie 6 beads in a circle.

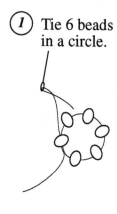

2 Add center.

3 Pick up 2 beads of the next daisy. Stitch as shown.

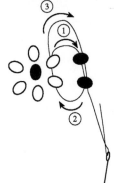

4 Pick up 4 beads to complete circle.

5 Add center.

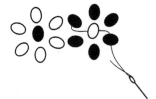

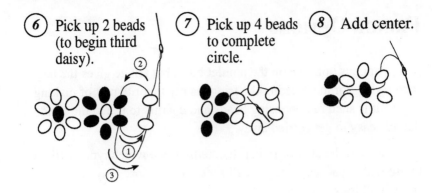

6 Pick up 2 beads (to begin third daisy).

7 Pick up 4 beads to complete circle.

8 Add center.

Repeat steps 3-8 until you have the desired length. Make daisies in as many colors as you wish.

FRINGE OPTIONS

Fringe is optional on the amulet bags, but fringe gives the bag such style. For me, making the fringe is my favorite part of making a bag. It is such fun choosing beads and charms to use in the fringe that it's easy to get carried away.

As with the chains, rather than telling you which type of fringe to use with a particular bag, I will give you options. Any type of fringe will look good on any bag.

STRAIGHT FRINGE

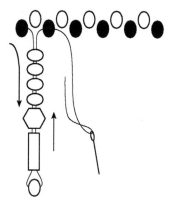

Straight fringe can all be the same length, or tapered. For a "V" taper add 3-4 seed beads to each fringe until you get to the center, then decrease.

KINKY FRINGE

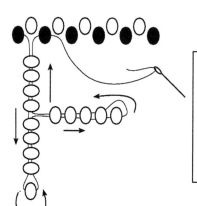

Add side fringe to the main fringe. Add as few or as many side fringe as you like.

26

LOOPED FRINGE #1

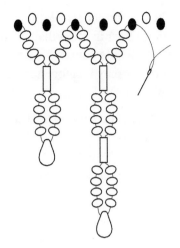

LOOPED FRINGE #2

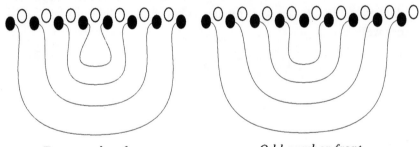

Even number front   *Odd number front*

LOOPED/STRAIGHT COMBINATION

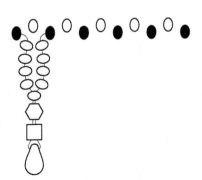

The top part of this fringe is a loop. The bottom portion is straight. Use large beads on the bottom portion and seed beads on the top.

Twisted Fringe

Thread on seed beads, the accent beads, and seed beads as shown by the illustration. Bear in mind that as you twist the fringe, it will shorten a little. Make allowances for this if you have a particular length in mind. It may be more accurate to measure the beads rather than count them.

The fringe beads should be snug against the body of the bag. Hold the side of the thread that is attached to the needle as close to the fringe beads as possible. Begin twisting the thread while keeping the beads close together. You will need to twist the thread several times.

When you bring the two ends together, they should twist around each other. Before bringing the needle through the body of the bag, allow the beadless part of the thread to untwist so you do not get a knot. While doing this, you MUST hold the thread against the beads. You do not want the beaded portion of the thread to unravel!

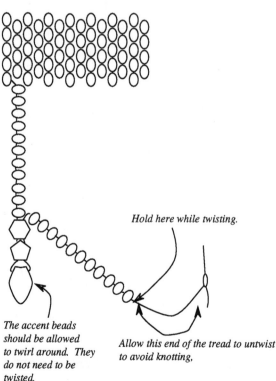

Hold here while twisting.

The accent beads should be allowed to twirl around. They do not need to be twisted.

Allow this end of the tread to untwist to avoid knotting.

28

Sometimes, no matter what you do, some thread shows at the top of the fringe. This is caused by the weight of the beads stretching the thread. You can hide this by making a "skirt". This also softens the appearance of the bottom of the bag. Add the skirt after the fringe is done.

Method 1

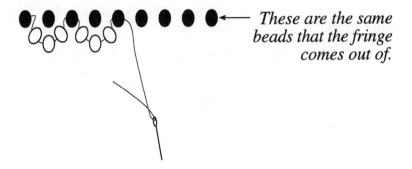

These are the same beads that the fringe comes out of.

Method 2

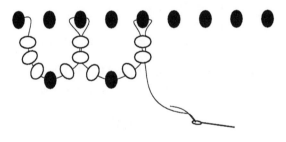

TIP

To keep thread from entangling in the fringe, wrap the fringe in tissue. It will save you a lot of time untangling thread from the fringe!

CLOSURES FOR PEYOTE STITCH BAGS

A closure is not necessary on these bags, however, if you would like one, it is easy to add.

LOOP/BEAD CLOSURE

You may need to extend the top of the bag so that the bead (button) used for a closure does not interfere with the design.

Sew a bead 6mm or larger on to the front top of the bag.

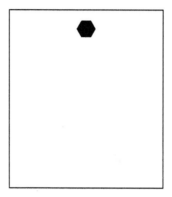

From the back, form a loop of seed beads large enough so that it can go over the bead in front, snugly. Reinforce several times for strength.

ATTACHED LID

An attached lid is very simple to make. I feel that they work the best for bags that have a peyote stitched strap. However, you can make the lid for bags with other types of straps, as you can see I have done with the Wizard bag. You just need to ensure that the lid can slide up far enough so that you can open it. Make the lid after you have completed the strap.

The lid needs to be slightly bigger than the bag so that it can slip over the beads of the bag. I have found that if you increase the "start" beads by eight for a bag made of delica beads, the lid will have a good fit. If you are using other types of beads such as round size 11^0 beads, or size 14^0, you will need to adjust this number. Simply add an even number of beads to the "start" beads, tie the beads into a circle and test the fit over the bag.

Plan for the lid by making sure that the lid will not cover any of the design. You can always extend the to of the bag by making several rows of background color. For example, on the Wizard bag, I extended the top by about 10 rows.

Additionally, if you make an edging for your bags as I do, you must leave off the edging for several of the top rows (the lid does not fit over edging well). The number of rows you leave the edging off of is dependent on how long your lid is.

Begin the lid in the same manner as you would begin a bag. Peyote stitch approximately 10 rows. Do not flatten, even if you have flattened the bag.

Slip this band over the bag. From either the front or the back, you will now continue with flat peyote stitch. How close you come to the edge will be dependent on the width of your strap.

Make the flat peyote stitch segment only as long as needed to meet the other side of the lid. The number of rows required is dependent on the type of beads that you use.

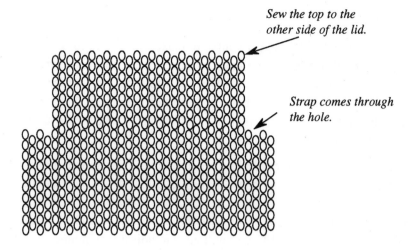

Sew the top to the other side of the lid.

Strap comes through the hole.

Buttonhole Closure

As with the lid closure, the top of the bag may need to be extended several rows so that the design does not get covered.

Begin by finding the center of the bag. Start a flat peyote extension 2 or 3 stitches to the left of center. Stitch as usual. Stop short of center the same distance as you started.

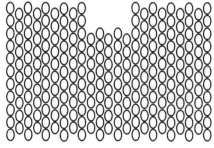

① *Front top of bag with flat peyote stitch extension.*

After 3 or 4 rows, you can bridge the gap.

FIRE SERPENT

FROG   CASH

GOLDEN GIRL   LUCKY CARD

HERON   PEACOCK

ORCA   PUFFIN

PETROGLYPH   TURTLE

SWINGING ON THE MOON   OVER THE MOON

WIZARD   MOON GODDESS

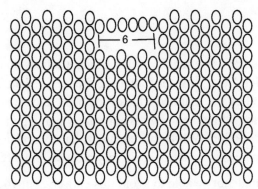

$\textcircled{2}$ *Bridge the gap by adding as many beads as there empty columns.*

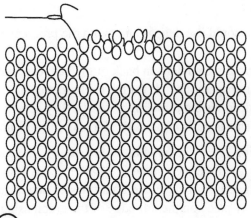

$\textcircled{3}$ *Continue with circular peyote stitch as usual*

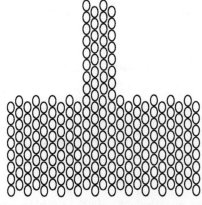

$\textcircled{4}$ *From the center of the back of the bag, make a tab of flat peyote stitch that will fit through the button hole. Pull the tab through the hole and sew a 4mm bead on the end to keep the tab from slipping out.*

Tips

1. If you are using regular round beads, (delicas do not have this problem) you may encounter the dreaded "slant". This is caused by the rounded edge of the bead moving out of position while the thread is constantly being pulled tight in one direction. While this change is hardly noticeable on a row by row basis, it makes itself very clear within a few rows.

    You may not be able to avoid this entirely, but you can certainly ease the slant by pulling the bag on opposite corners in a direction opposite to the direction of the slant to straighten the bag out.

    Or you could use delicas and avoid the problem entirely.

2. Keep your step downs in back of the bag, especially when using transparent beads for the background. The step downs are indeed visible through the beads, they appear as a diagonal line. This is quite unpleasant if it should show up in the front.

    Additionally, by keeping the step downs in the back, keeping your place on the graph will be easier as the design won't be broken up into "before and after the step down" halves. I mark my place on the left edge of the graph using just the first two columns and never get lost.

3. Ease your tension **slightly** while working the third row (the first row after you pick up the "start" beads), especially if you plan on flattening the bag. If your tension is too tight, the edges of the bag will have a tendency to curve upwards.

4. If you have a hard time starting those bags with the designs that go all the way to the top, start by making 2 rows of just the background color, then begin the design as you would with the other bags. If you do not knot in the beginning, you can pull out the first few rows.

    Another easy way to deal with the problem, would be to work from the bottom up if the design doesn't go to the bottom.

5. For fuller fringe on bags made with delica beads, try to use size 11^0 beads if you can find a good match.

6. For even richer fringe, put fringe on both the front of the bag **and** the back, as I did with the Grapes bag. Use the beads you want to show the most for the front.

7. Stretch Nymo thread (especially for the fringe and straps). Heavy fringe will eventually stretch the thread leaving unsightly gaps between the body and the top of the fringe. If you have especially heavy fringe, I recommend that you make a skirt around the bottom of the bag.

8. Sign your name or initials on the back of the bag. You put a lot of time and skill into making the bag, you deserve the privilege of signing your art work!!

9. **Buy beads, LOTS OF BEADS!!** My best moments of creativity hits late at night. Nothing is worse than needing beads to create what you have in mind. The bead stores in my area are not open into the wee hours, nor do they have emergency numbers. So I have learned to stock up as much as my budget can afford.

10. Label beads by the inventory number (and store), so that when you run out you can easily get more. This is especially useful for mail order.

11. Last, but not least, have **fun** while making these bags. Experiment with colors, make wild, funky fringe, take the basic design and play with it. I have kept the basic design elements fairly simple for the purposes of writing directions and clarity, but that doesn't mean you can't add special surface embellishments, or other detailing.

PATTERNS

Remember that these patterns show only the front of the bag. The "start" number given for each of the bags is for the entire number of beads needed for the first two rows of the bag (rows 1 & 2 of the front times 2). This is given to save you a little time counting.

At the request of a good friend (hi Gail!) I've also included the inventory numbers of the delica beads that I used in making these bags after the name of the color. Please note that my color descriptions are **not** the same as the manufacturers' color descriptions. This is so that if you do not wish to use the delicas, you won't have to figure out what color some of those interesting names are. I believe that most store use the same numbers. If not they should, so that there can be consistency for the ease of ordering. This is by no means a requirement for you to use the same colors or even the same beads. But for those of you who like my color combinations, you won't be agonizing trying to figure out what colors I used.

BIRD

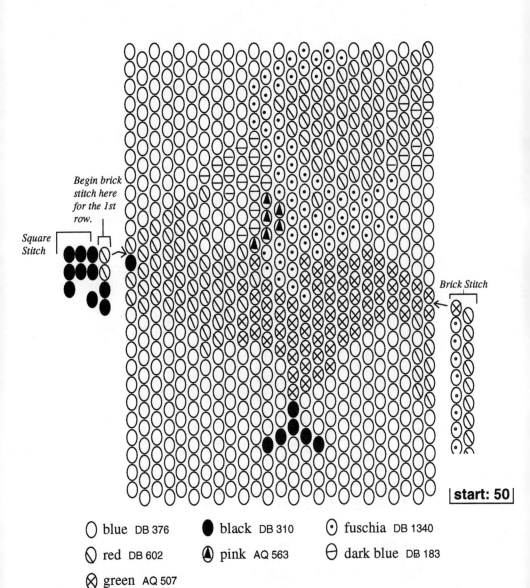

Begin brick stitch here for the 1st row.

Square Stitch

Brick Stitch

start: 50

○ blue DB 376 ● black DB 310 ⊙ fuschia DB 1340

◑ red DB 602 ◭ pink AQ 563 ⊖ dark blue DB 183

⊗ green AQ 507

start: 50

37

CARDINAL

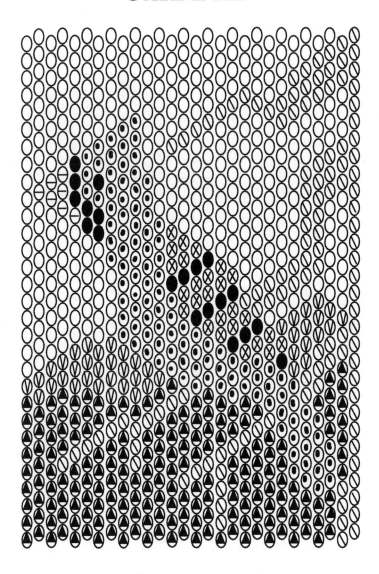

O blue DB 83   Ø brown AQ 702   ⊗ dark red DB 723

● black DB 310   ◭ green DB 327   ◉ red DB 362

⊖ orange DB 744   Ⓥ white DB 66

start: 56

38

CASH

O green DB 373   ● gold DB 310   ⊙ cream DB 352

start: 54

CELTIC CROSS

● black DB 310   ◊ green DB 605   ○ gold DB 310

start: 78

40

Deco

- ● black DB 310
- ⊙ matte gold DB 331
- ⊗ gold AQ 551
- ⊖ burgandy AQ 503
- ⊘ matte burgandy AQ 703

start: 50

FIRE SERPENT

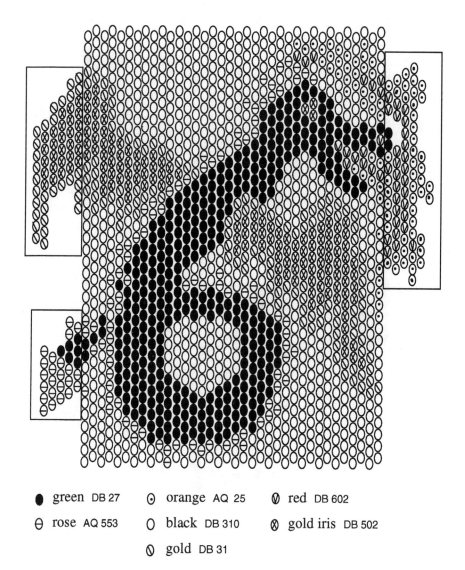

- ● green DB 27
- ⊖ rose AQ 553
- ☉ orange AQ 25
- ○ black DB 310
- Ⓝ gold DB 31
- Ⓥ red DB 602
- ⊗ gold iris DB 502

Boxed areas are done in Brick Stitch

start: 72

FROG

◯ blue DB 218	⊙ green DB 754	⬤ black DB 310
⊘ leaf green DB 46	⊗ yellow DB 160	ⓥ dark green DB 327

start: 58

GOLDEN GIRL

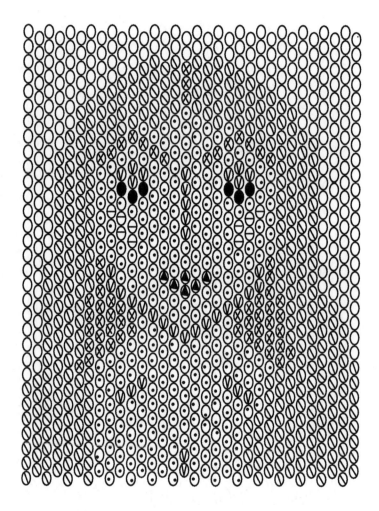

⊗	matte gold DB 331	▲	red DB 62	●	brown AQ 702
ⓥ	dark peach DB 206	⊖	rose DB 379	⊙	peach DB 354
○	bronze iris DB 29	ⓥ	gold AQ 551		

start: 64

GRAPES

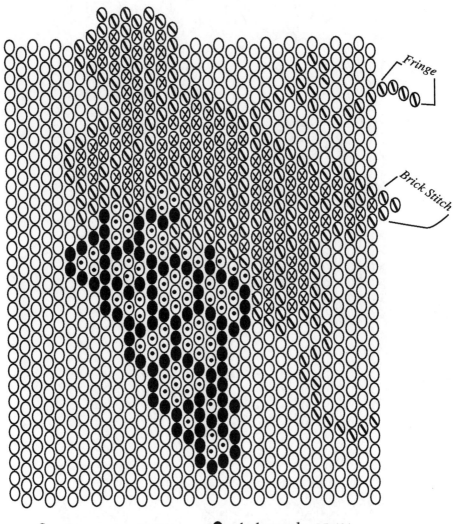

- ◯ champagne DB 901
- ◉ light purple DB 906
- ⊗ light green DB 754
- ● dark purple DB 461
- ◍ dark green AQ 507

start: 64

45

HERON

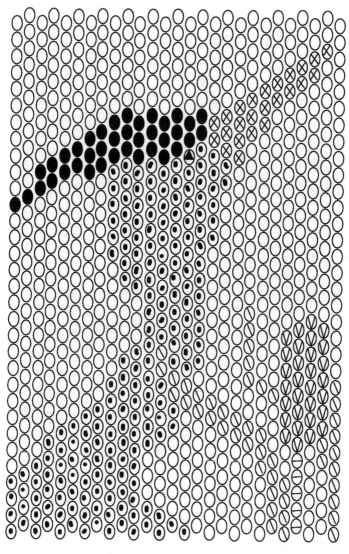

◯	light blue DB 83	Ⓥ	dark brown AQ 614	⊗	orange DB 651
⊙	white DB 221	⊖	light brown DB 653	◓	black DB 310
Ⓝ	green DB 655	⬤	dark gray DB 697		

start: 54

46

LUCKY CARD

○ white DB 202   ● black DB 310

start: 56

MOON GODDESS

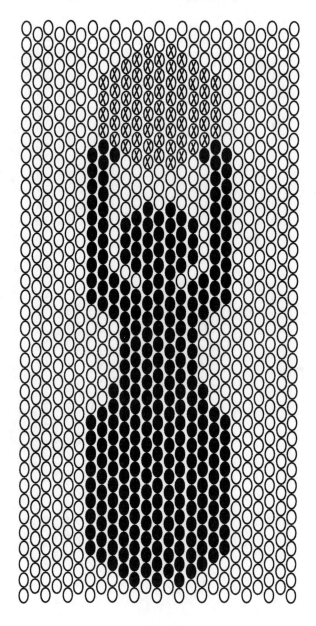

Ⓧ white DB 221   ● gold DB 42   ○ purple DB 135

start: 50

ORCA

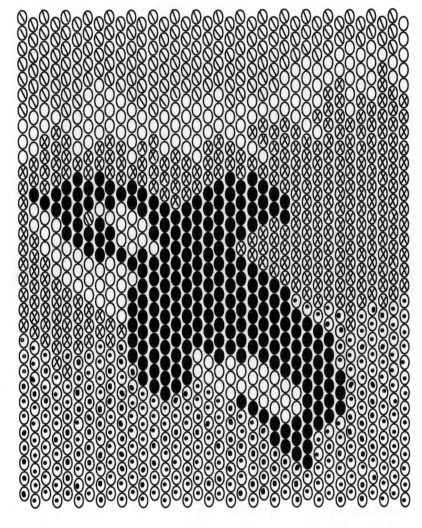

● black DB 310   ◉ dark blue DB 905   ◐ bronze DB 12

○ white DB 200   ◑ sky blue DB 83   ⊗ green DB 327

start: 72

OVER THE MOON

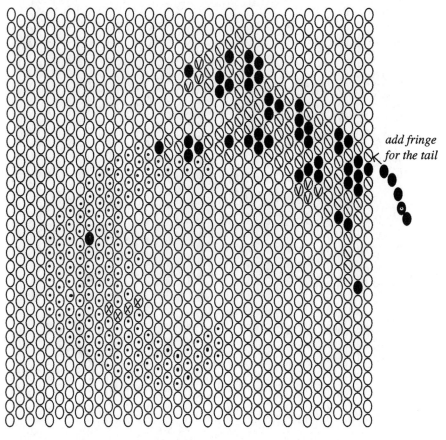

add fringe
for the tail

◯	dark blue AQ 248	◍	white DB 200	⬗	peach DB 206
⬤	black DB 310	⊙	yellow DB 412	⊗	red DB 602

start: 74

PARROT

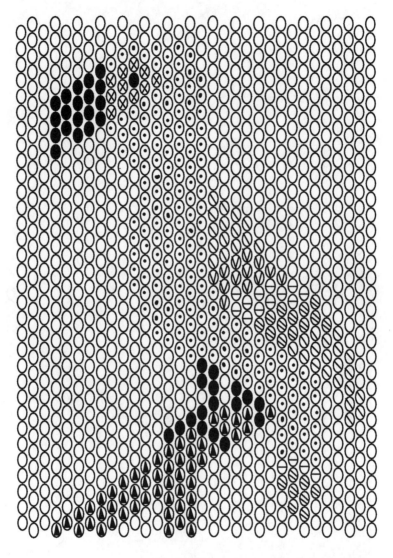

◯ silver DB 41	◭ tan DB 653	⊙ red DB 723
● black DB 310	⊘ blue DB 165	⊘ dark red DB 378
⊘ yellow DB 160	⊗ white DB 200	⊖ green DB 655

start: 64

PEACOCK

O white luster DB 109   ● bronze DB 12   ϴ orange DB 702

● royal blue DB 165   ⊘ green DB 27

start: 72

PETROGLYPH

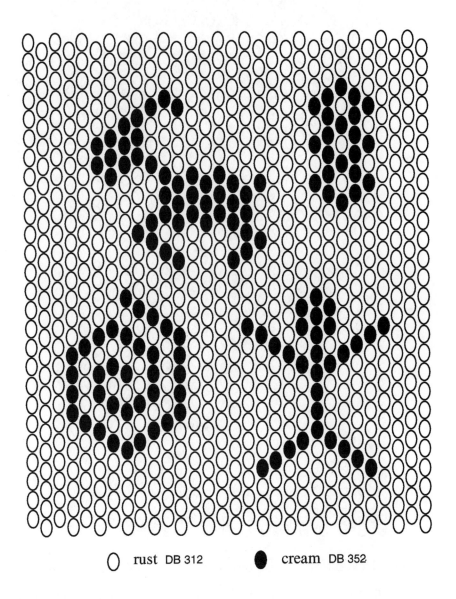

◯ rust DB 312 ⬤ cream DB 352

start: 60

PUFFIN

● matte black DB 310	⊖ brown DB 380	◗ dark green DB 327
⊗ black DB 10	⊙ white DB 351	⑩ dark blue DB 165
○ light blue DB 905	◌ orange DB 744	◓ yellow DB 903

start: 68

54

Fish for Puffin

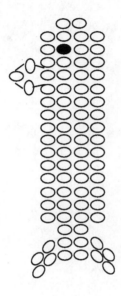

Make the fish by using square stitch for the body, a 3-bead loop for the fin, and brick stitch for the tail.

The four beads on either side of the tail are made by using brick stitch. By forcing 2 beads where there should be 1 on the top row of brick stitch, will cause the tail to angle into a "V".

Make 2 half fishes to sew into the puffin's beak.

Size 14 seed beads are recommended for the fish.

SWINGING ON THE MOON

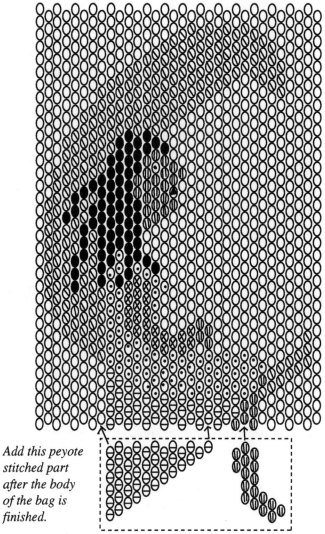

Add this peyote stitched part after the body of the bag is finished.

O   black iris DB 2

Ø   white opal DB 221

☉   royal blue DB 165

◕   red DB 602

 θ   tranparent blue DB 706

◍   peach DB 206

●   brown DB 612

start: 64

56

TURTLE

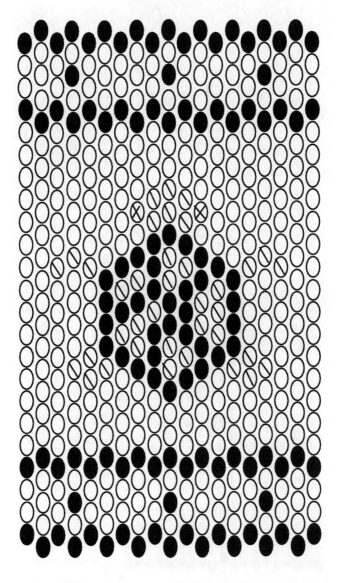

● dark green AQ 507   ⊘ medium green DB 152

⊗ orange AQ 25   ○ light green DB 903

start: 38

WIZARD

Robe extension to be added after bottom of bag is sewn together.

● purple DB 610   ◯ bronze DB 22   ⊙ peach DB 206

◐ white DB 211   ⊗ crystal DB 109   ◓ black DB 310

start: 60

58

UPPERCASE LETTERS

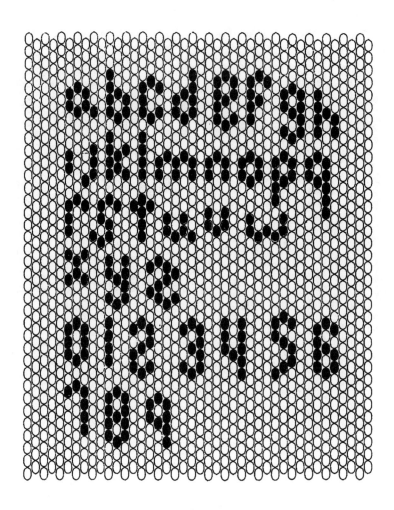

BLANK PEYOTE STITCH GRAPH

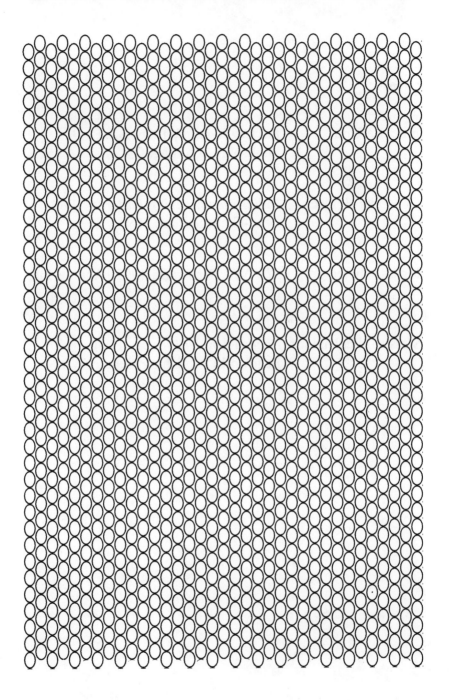

Sources of Inspiration

Elbe, Barbara   *Back to Beadin',* 1996, B.E.E.
Publishing, Redding, CA

Goodhue, Horace   *Indian Beadweaving Patterns,* 1989,
Bead-Craft, St Paul, MN

Moss, Scherer   *The New Beadwork,* 1992 , Abrams Inc,
NY

Stessin, Nicolette   *Beaded Amulet Purses ,* 1994,
Beadworld Publishing, Seattle, WA

TRY THESE FANTASTIC EARRING DESIGNS!

Each book features different image designs for Comanche Weave earrings. You'll be able to find a complimentary design for most of the amulet bag designs in one of these four books.

Earring Designs by Sig Vol. 1 — Includes: Bear, Kokopelli, Cat and Mermaid.

Earring Designs by Sig Vol. 2 — Includes: Eagle, Fishes, Merlin, and Owl.

Earring Designs by Sig Vol. 3 — Includes: Angel, Crescent Moon, Santa, and Bouquet.

An Earful of Designs — Includes: Hummingbird, Fire Serpent, Japanese Crane, and Tiger.

And Don't Forget Sig's First Amulet Bag Book,
The Magical Amulet Bag

ORDER FORM

Name:_____

Address:_____

_____

Phone_____

Earring Designs by Sig Vol.1   _____ X $8.95_____

Earring Designs by Sig Vol. 2   _____ X $8.95_____

Earring Designs by Sig Vol. 3   _____ X $9.95_____

An Earful of Designs   _____ X $9.95_____

The Magical Amulet Bag   _____ X $10.95_____

The Magical Amulet Bag Vol.2   _____ X $11.95_____

Shipping: Add $2 for 1 book, and $1 for each
                    additional book
CA residents must add 8.25% sales tax   _____

                                        TOTAL   _____

Please send check or money order to:
        The Beaded Bear
        P.O. Box 110894
        Campbell, CA 95011
        (408) 379-8647
Prices and availability subject to change without notice